THE IRA TRUST

Turning Inherited Retirement Accounts
Into a Financial Dynasty

Jeffrey G. Marsocci, Esq.

Domestic Partner Publishing, LLC

Note regarding legal counsel

As with any product, it is important to be clear about its intended purpose and use to avoid any misunderstandings. Specifically with writings about legal issues, it is noted that these materials are not a substitute for competent legal counsel. The contents of this book are instead written to provide information about common estate planning problems faced by domestic partners, and it is designed for general educational purposes only. The contents of this book are not to be construed as legal advice, and no attorney-client privilege exists between the reader and the author and/or publisher. In addition, laws change frequently, and therefore you also are urged to speak with an attorney about changes in the law that may affect you.

Circular 230 Disclosure: To ensure compliance with requirements imposed by the Internal Revenue Service, unless specifically indicated otherwise, any tax advice contained in this communication (including any accompanying literature) was not intended or written to be used, and cannot be used, for the purpose of avoiding tax-related penalties or promoting, marketing, or recommending to another party any tax-related matter addressed herein. For specific legal advice, you are urged to contact an attorney in your state or jurisdiction.

About the Author

Jeffrey G. Marsocci was born in Fort Worth, Texas, and raised in Lincoln, Rhode Island, where he graduated from Mount Saint Charles Academy High School. He received his Bachelor's degree in Business from Hofstra University, and two years later earned his law degree from the same university.

In 2004, he received a Certificate Degree in Non-Profit Management from Duke University, and has earned his Legal Master of Estate Preservation designation from the *Abts Institute for Estate Preservation*. Jeff also serves as a member of the Legal Council for The Estate Plan, a nationally recognized estate preservation company headed by Henry Abts, trust guru and author of *The Living Trust*.

Mr. Marsocci has led his own firm in Raleigh, North Carolina, since 1996, focusing on the areas of Wills, Trusts and Life & Estate Planning with a concentration on helping his clients plan ahead to avoid problems rather than clean them up afterwards. He is also a founding member of The National Institute for Domestic Partner Estate Planning, and he frequently participates in programs to educate attorneys, financial advisors and accountants on estate planning issues.

Jeff and his wife Kathleen are active Kiwanis members, working with the college-based service organization Circle K throughout North Carolina and South Carolina. Jeff and Kathy also each received the President's Call to Service Award for performing more than 4,000 hours of service during their lifetimes.

This book is dedicated to those people who care enough to plan ahead now so that their loved ones can prosper for a lifetime.

TABLE OF CONTENTS

Introduction

There are tremendous benefits available to people who plan ahead, and even more benefits are available for the heirs we left behind if things are handled properly. Unfortunately, these benefits are not available to those who let the opportunities slip them by or act rashly before talking to knowledgeable professionals. There is no more advantageous area for financial gain for beneficiaries than properly handling the inheritance of retirement accounts. There is also no more dangerous area for financial loss for beneficiaries than inheriting a retirement account and mishandling it.

And all it takes to "mishandle" inheriting a retirement account is cashing a check.

And that's what most people are inclined to do when they get a check, and that is what most people do. That simple act of cashing or depositing the inheritance check from a loved one's retirement account can mean the difference between hundreds of thousands of dollars in immediate income taxes or millions of dollars in tax-deferred financial dynasty lasting a lifetime.

While some of the techniques and strategies reviewed in this book may sound simple, they take an educated and experienced professional to help set things up correctly the first time because even small mistakes can be costly and irreversible. Your heirs may never get a second chance to maximize their inheritance.

For now, please read on, and, more importantly, act upon what you read.

Chapter One:
The Income Tax System

One of the greatest income tax benefits "bestowed" on people by the government is the ability to fund retirement accounts and deduct the contributions from their income tax. Income taxes are then paid when amounts are withdrawn from these accounts, presumably when they are in a lower tax bracket after retirement begins. One of the biggest tax burdens falls upon these retirement accounts when the owner passes on, with all of the amounts in the retirement accounts counted as income to the beneficiary. And then the remainder is taxed *again* as part of the deceased person's taxable estate. In some cases, as much as 75% of the account can be lost to what amounts to double taxation.

Until recently, married couples had the only tax relief in the form of a "rollover." When one spouse passed on leaving their account to their spouse, 100% is exempt from estate taxes anyway and the surviving spouse could additionally put the retirement funds into their own retirement accounts *without paying any income taxes until they took the money out.*

Now, thanks in large part to lobbying efforts from various tax reform and equal opportunity groups, Congress took action to extend at least partial equality to individuals and unmarried couples, including benefits for children and other beneficiaries. Now people can name *any* individual or individuals as beneficiary on their retirement accounts and, provided they take the right steps, can reduce and greatly defer taxes.

Before delving into the specifics about how inherited retirement accounts can avoid unnecessary taxes, let's take a look at how retirement accounts in general are taxed during life and after death.

Taxes Paid on Retirement Accounts During Life

Taxpayers have certain rules that apply to retirement accounts, whether they are Individual Retirement Accounts, 401ks, 403bs, and many other accounts. We will not get into all of the different kinds and permutations in this report, and instead if you have specific questions about your specific retirement accounts, please speak to a financial professional. The main kinds of accounts we will deal with in this report are the typical retirement accounts where you place wages into the retirement account, up to a certain limit, deduct those contributions from your income taxes, and then pay taxes on all money coming out of your account after retirement.

Unlike many other financial and investment accounts in the U.S., retirement accounts are *only* held by individuals and *can not* be owned jointly with another person. Therefore, income taxes during life are paid by the individual when they take money out and not spread among two or more people when filing taxes. The only exception to this is that while married couples can only have one of them separately own each retirement account, they can report the income on a joint tax return.

Retirement accounts and the legislation setting up the rules were designed to allow people to defer paying income taxes on amounts contributed to the account (again, up to a limit) and then tax those accounts when the money is taken out during retirement. There are three big benefits to these accounts during life. First, the money earned during working years is taxed less because of the deductions gained by putting money aside for retirement. For many individuals, it is the higher tax brackets that really put a dent in their income, and being able to take deductions while earning wages can greatly lower that tax bracket and the amount of income taxes paid.

Second, money does not just sit in an account remaining static and will hopefully grow. It can be invested in stocks, bonds and make gains and losses over time with the market like any other security. In the alternative, retirement money in these accounts can be placed into interest bearing accounts like savings accounts, or maybe even government bonds. There are also many other private, public and governmental investments that retirement accounts can hold *In all cases, there are no taxable gains or losses on these retirement accounts.* Since every dollar coming out during retirement is taxable as income, there are no income taxes or capital gains taxes on investments within the account while it grows.

For example, if John T. Axpayer puts $10,000 into a retirement account in 2007 and that earns 5% interest during 2008, that $500 of gain is not reported as income, it is not reported as capital gains, and in fact it is not reported at all. There is simply $10,500 in that account. Assuming John is 65 when he puts the money in and takes out $250 during 2010 when he is 67, he simply reports that $250 on his income tax return.

Third, while it is presumed that taxpayers earn more while they are working and thus need the tax deductions to avoid higher tax brackets, it is also presumed that there is a benefit to taking money out during retirement years because taxpayers are usually in lower tax brackets. Meanwhile, all of the money in the account grows tax-deferred. It is because taxpayers want to leave money in the account to grow and therefore avoid taking money out to avoid the additional taxes that there are also required minimum distributions set when account holders turn 70½.

Summary

There are significant income tax deductions for funding a retirement account during working years, and that money can be invested in various securities, bonds, and other public, private and government investments. But eventually those assets have to be withdrawn and then are taxed as income. In the next chapter, we will discuss how the government forces money to be withdrawn in the form of required minimum distributions.

Chapter Two:
Required Minimum Distributions, Income Taxes, and Death Taxes

"I'm sorry," the cheery older woman said, holding her husband's hand, "I don't understand what kind of tax problem we could have. We don't have that much money. We don't have 'an estate.' Do we?"

The attorney Andy Cook looked up from the list of assets and to the couple. "Actually, yes, you do," Andy said. "At least the IRS would say so. While there is not a lot in cash or mutual funds, you actually have a substantial amount of land and property, and your retirement accounts are pretty large as well. In all, you have about $3.5 million in assets, and those retirement accounts would be subject to estate taxes and income taxes."

While his wife Alice looked a little stunned at the amount, Doug stared at Andy, a little hardness in his expression. "Look, we've earned every penny we have," he said. "We worked hard. I didn't inherit piles of money. I took a big part of my paycheck each week and put some in retirement and some aside to buy rental properties. It was the smart thing to do. We just paid off the mortgages on the last property, and now you're telling me if something happened to me and my wife that my family could lose a lot of it to taxes?"

"Fortunately, we can work with your financial advisor and find some creative ways to take care of the taxes," Andy said. "The biggest problem would happen if we did nothing. Your heirs would be forced to either sell off the properties or drain those retirement accounts, incurring heft income taxes at the same time. In

fact, according to my calculations, if your children wanted to keep the rental properties in the family instead of selling them off, they would lose about 70 percent of your retirement accounts to pay the taxes. But to avoid that here's what I think we should do..."

While there are tremendous tax deductions for retirement account contributions and tremendous tax deferred growth on money inside the account, there is a point where the government wants its money to come out and be taxed as income. There are two main times the money must come out of the accounts, at least without the right planning, and those are during life after a certain age and then upon death.

Income Taxes Paid During life

According to the same federal laws that allow tax deductions and tax deferred growth, that point is 70½ years of age. When a person turns 70½, the government says people who have retirement accounts must start taking money out of their accounts.

While not entirely accurate, the easiest way to understand required minimum distributions is to say that you must take out an equal share of your retirement account each year depending on your estimated life expectancy. For example, if a person 70.5 has a life expectancy (according to IRS tables) of 85.5, then they must take out approximately 1/15th of their account that year. The next year when there are 14 years of life left (again, presumed under IRS tables), then 1/14th must be taken out and taxed as income.

Again, that is a simplification of the distribution rules. The fact is the IRS has tables and factors of life expectancy that determine the mandatory distribution each year starting with age 70½.

Some other general rules surrounding most retirement accounts are:

- while there are required minimum distributions at age 70½, more can be withdrawn without penalties (but these funds are also considered taxable income)

- funds can not be withdrawn from a retirement account until at least age 59½ without a penalty

- Every dollar that comes out is taxed as income

In many cases, people will accumulate and accumulate funds in retirement accounts tax-deferred. However, this leads to some huge potential distributions (and taxes) for people who saved heavily during working years but did not start taking out money early enough when they could do so without penalties.

Here are some examples of Required Minimum Distributions for someone 70½ in 2009 and the corresponding distributions coupled with an assumed growth rate of 6% through age 100.

Year	Age	Distribution	Balance	Cumulative Distributions
2009	70	$18,248	$510,657	$18,248
2010	71	$19,270	$520,870	$37,518
2011	72	$20,346	$530,555	$57,865
2012	73	$21,480	$539,620	$79,345
2013	74	$22,673	$547,963	$102,018
2014	75	$23,929	$555,477	$125,946
2015	76	$25,249	$562,042	$151,195
2016	77	$26,511	$567,662	$177,707
2017	78	$27,964	$572,080	$205,670

Turning Inherited Retirement Accounts Into a Financial Dynasty

2018	79	$29,337	$575,307	$235,008
2019	80	$30,765	$577,215	$265,773
2020	81	$32,247	$577,666	$298,019
2021	82	$33,782	$576,518	$331,801
2022	83	$35,369	$573,617	$367,170
2023	84	$37,008	$568,806	$404,178
2024	85	$38,433	$562,196	$442,611
2025	86	$39,872	$553,663	$482,483
2026	87	$41,318	$543,086	$523,801
2027	88	$42,763	$530,343	$566,564
2028	89	$44,195	$515,316	$610,759
2029	90	$45,203	$498,320	$655,962
2030	91	$46,141	$479,310	$702,103
2031	92	$46,991	$458,258	$749,094
2032	93	$47,735	$435,154	$796,829
2033	94	$47,819	$410,575	$844,648
2034	95	$47,741	$384,604	$892,389
2035	96	$47,482	$357,349	$939,871
2036	97	$47,020	$328,949	$986,891
2037	98	$46,331	$299,575	$1,033,222
2038	99	$44,713	$270,154	$1,077,935
2039	100	$42,882	$240,909	$1,120,816

Turning Inherited Retirement Accounts Into a Financial Dynasty

As you can see, the account pays a lot out over time, but the federal government insists on a growing share of the account being taken out as each year passes. And every dollar is counted as taxable income in the year distributed. Over a 40-year period with 6% growth, the $500,000 retirement account pays out more than $1.1 million and still has more than $240,000 left in the account. As you can see, the tax deferred growth is fantastic, but eventually the money is forced out by these required minimum distributions.

Taxes Paid on Retirement Accounts at Death

Most people enjoy the benefits of being able to put away money which gives them an income tax deduction and grows tax-deferred, but they hesitate to take the money out because it's taxable at that point. The problem is that when you combine the taxable account with the most of the account could be lost to taxes when the owner passes on.

Whenever a person passes on, any property left to a non-spouse, including the balances in retirement accounts, become part of that person's taxable estate. That federal death tax rate and the exemptions depend on the year and the corresponding exemptions. For example, if an unmarried person passes on in 2008 with a $1 million house, a $1 million mutual fund, and a $1 million IRA, they would have a taxable estate of $3 million and have a federal estate tax bill of $435,000. The same person passing on in 2009 with a $3.5 million exemption would have no federal death taxes, but that person passing on in 2011 with $1 million in exemptions would have $905,000 in federal death taxes.

In addition, upon death retirement accounts have *income taxes* due except in a few situations (which we will discuss later). So if in 2008 that $1 million account is inherited by your son and they cash the check, your son now has $1 million in income on top of their own income, meaning $350,000 or so is lost to income taxes as well. If there were no retirement accounts, the $2 million in other assets would have been inherited without death taxes and without income taxes, and therefore the IRA actually had $785,000 of the $1 million lost to taxes. Please note that there is no 15% "penalty" for the beneficiary cashing out the inherited retirement account because the beneficiary is below retirement age. That penalty only counts for withdrawing early from *their own* retirement account.

Let's take a look at a specific example in 2011 when the estate tax exemptions are only $1 million. If Larry is John's father, and Larry has an IRA worth $500,000, a house worth $500,000, and a piece of commercial real estate worth $1,000,000, and Larry passes on in 2011, he has a $2 million taxable estate. That equals $435,000 in estate taxes. In addition, if John earns $75,000 per year and simply cashes the check the IRA plan administrator mailed to him, then John has $177,123 to pay in income taxes versus $12,856 if he did not cash the check. This means that John inheriting $500,000 in IRA assets and not handling it properly resulted in $164,267 in extra taxes above and beyond the $435,000 already imposed on the estate. In this example, if the IRA money were used to pay the taxes, it was completely wiped out and John still has to find another $99,267 in cash to pay those taxes or be forced to sell the house or the parcel of property.

But inheriting a retirement account does not have to incur all of the income taxes all at once. As we'll see in the next chapter, there are solutions that can allow for great deferrals and growth in taxes.

Chapter Three:
Stretching an Inherited Retirement Account

Matt's palms were getting sweaty, and a dull panic started to run through him sending an involuntary chill up his spine. He was sitting down to Sunday dinner at his brother's house, the first one where all three of the children got together since Dad passed on, and he was starting to see he may have made a huge mistake.

"I was a little shocked when I got the check from the brokerage firm," James said to his siblings as he passed the salad bowl. "I started wondering what I could do with all of that money. Thankfully I talked with Margie before doing anything."

Their sister Cindy adjusted the bib on her youngest child and turned to James. "Yeah, thanks for turning me on to her," Cindy said. "She's been helping us out with our own retirement planning and life insurance since you recommended her a year ago, and she told me as soon as she got off the phone with you she called me. Thank God I didn't just cash the check. I was actually going to go to the bank later that day. We would have been killed with income taxes and lose all of those other tax benefits"

It was too much for Matt. "Wait a minute," he said. "What are you talking about?"

"The retirement account check from Dad's brokerage company," James said questioningly. "When I talked to Margie she went over the check and the letter from the brokerage company, and she told me if I cashed the check it would all

be taxed in one year. We set it up so it would only have to be withdrawn a little at a time."

"And it could grow each year without taxes like my 401k and my husband's IRA," Cindy chimed in. "Wait a minute… you just back from Las Vegas. Did you cash the check to pay for the trip for you and Valerie?"

Matt just sat back and sighed. James looked a little bit angry but a lot more pitying. "You never did call Margie last year when I told you to, did you?" James said. "And now you'll have a about a hundred thousand dollars in income taxes to pay next April 15."

"Matt?" Cindy asked her brother. "Just how much of that check did you already spend?"

There are inheritance solutions for retirement accounts that people can take advantage of, namely "stretching" the retirement account. While the retirement account is still counted as part of the deceased person's taxable estate, instead of all of the income taxes on the account being due right away, the beneficiary or beneficiaries can transfer the funds into an "Inherited Individual Retirement Account (IRA)." Now the beneficiary can spread the distributions, and the income taxes, over their lifetime. While this is not a tax free retirement account and only a tax-deferred one, it is definitely a step in the right direction. However (and there is always a "however"), there are restrictions and the account must be set up the right way. They are:

- The beneficiary on the account must be listed as an individual (or a special type of trust discussed below)

- The funds must be transferred directly to the Inherited IRA Account

- The beneficiary must withdraw a minimum amount each year, all of which is taxed as income

Turning Inherited Retirement Accounts Into a Financial Dynasty

First, the retirement account must list the beneficiary as the recipient on any beneficiary designation form. It can not be "estate" or even a revocable living trust. In some cases, the revocable living trust can be the beneficiary if it has certain "pass through" language. (Because of the huge tax burdens that can be triggered by a mistake in this area, be sure to use an attorney experienced in life and estate planning—a mistake can cost hundreds of thousands of dollars or more.)

The next and most critical restriction is that the funds must be transferred by the beneficiary directly into an inherited IRA account. *Be sure to speak to a financial professional before doing anything.*

Most people will first try to settle an estate by themselves without using an attorney or financial advisor. Usually the financial institution holding the retirement account only needs a death certificate before they write a check to a named beneficiary. The beneficiary will usually do what anyone does with a large check written to them—they'll deposit it into an account. If this happens, game over. All of the income taxes will be due with the beneficiary's next round of tax returns. And going to see a financial advisor afterwards probably will not help. If not a direct account-to-account transfer into the inherited IRA account, at the very least the check should be given to the financial advisor establishing the account for deposit into the inherited IRA account.

Finally, part of the legislation requires that the beneficiary withdraw a minimum amount each year. While in retirement age, this is the required minimum distributions for the original account owner.that start at 70½ years of age and they must start withdrawing funds in amounts determined by IRS tables over the course of their life expectancy. Again, note that *more* than the minimum can be taken out each year; it is just mandatory that the minimum be withdrawn and taxed in each year.

For an inherited IRA, the rules are slightly different than the typical retirement account in that the beneficiary must start withdrawing the funds over their life expectancy *starting right away*, regardless of their age. So a 50 year old beneficiary would have to withdraw roughly equal amounts over the next 35 years or so until the account is depleted. There are no penalties for withdrawing the funds even at a pre-retirement age on inherited IRA accounts even though on their personal retirement accounts there would be penalties for withdrawing before age 59½. These forced distributions do take away some flexibility from financial planning, but the money saved by not having to pay all of the income taxes up front can be astounding.

For example, if John and Fred are cousins, both age 45, and John has a 401k with $500,000 when he prematurely passes on leaving his account to Fred, Fred can either take $500,000 of income on top of his own income that year or he can placed the $500,000 in an inherited IRA. If Fred earns $75,000 a year, and he just takes the check from John's retirement account and deposits it into his checking account, his federal income taxes (using standard deductions) would be about $178,000 versus roughly $13,000 by using the inherited IRA to shelter the $500,000. Using the inherited IRA, Fred can actually turn the $500,000 into about $2,073,000 in distributions if he lives to life expectancy (using 6% annual interest). In addition, if John instead had left the account to a 6 year old grandchild, the money in the account would exponentially increase. The same $500,000 account would generate more than $10,000,000 over the child's lifetime. If the money remaining after taxes on each of those distributions is invested rather than spent, the money generated can be enormous.

Here is an example of a 40 year old inheriting a $500,000 account and the amounts being spread over their lifetime.

Age	Required Minimum Distribution	Account Balance
40	$11,468	$513,532
41	$12,055	$527,154
42	$12,672	$540,840
43	$13,321	$554,561
44	$14,004	$568,284
45	$14,722	$581,976
46	$15,478	$595,597
47	$16,273	$609,104
48	$17,110	$622,449
49	$17,990	$635,582
50	$18,916	$648,445
51	$19,891	$660,976
52	$20,917	$673,108
53	$21,997	$684,766
54	$23,134	$695,871
55	$24,331	$706,333
56	$25,592	$716,058
57	$26,919	$724,941
58	$28,318	$732,870
59	$29,791	$739,722
60	$31,344	$745,364
61	$32,981	$749,652
62	$34,706	$752,428
63	$36,526	$753,524
64	$38,445	$752,755
65	$40,471	$749,922
66	$42,609	$744,809
67	$44,868	$737,182
68	$47,255	$726,785
69	$49,780	$713,345
70	$52,452	$696,560
71	$55,283	$676,106

72	$58,285	$651,626
73	$61,474	$622,733
74	$64,868	$589,002
75	$68,489	$549,963
76	$72,364	$505,098
77	$76,530	$453,823
78	$81,040	$395,474
79	$85,973	$329,275
80	$91,465	$254,274
81	$97,798	$169,190
82	$105,744	$71,905
83	$75,501	$0

$1,831,150

As you can see, there are tremendous accumulations that can be spread out over a lifetime. This can reduce the overall tax burden, allow money to grow inside the account tax deferred, and turn a sizeable inheritance in the year of death into a lifetime of income more than triple the original inheritance.

But there is one, big problem with this setup… most people who inherit retirement money squander it.

By some accounts, nearly ninety percent of inherited retirement account funds are gone within two years. Gone. Yes, minimum distributions must come out of an inherited retirement account, but those are only minimums… the beneficiaries can drain the money as quickly as they wish. Usually long before it was intended to be drained. But there is a solution to preserve the retirement account money, allow it to grow tax deferred, and keep anything other than the minimum distributions from coming out of the retirement account. It is called an IRA Trust.

Chapter Four:
The IRA Trust

"I think I understand what you are saying," the gentleman said, adjusting his button-down sweater. "The tax benefits of, what did you call it, stretching, the retirement account are substantial. But all of this depends on my son doing the right thing and only taking the minimum out each year, right?"

John Alford was sitting at the table with his attorney and financial advisor, and they were reviewing the distribution plans for his estate. His revocable living trust was in place, and that would handle almost all of his property going to his son. Almost all of the property. His retirement accounts were another matter because of income taxes.

"That's right," Margie the financial advisor said. "Your son can inherit your retirement account, place the funds into an Inherited IRA, and then by only taking the minimum amount each year it can grow substantially over time tax-deferred."

"I'm not so sure he'll do the right thing," Mr. Alford said, looking at Andy. "My son doesn't live extravagantly, but he does tend to spend money when he gets it. I'm just worried he'll keep turning to the retirement account like it's an ATM. That's why I put some restrictions into my revocable living trust to make sure the money is not wasted."

"Well, we could list your revocable living trust as the beneficiary of your retirement accounts," Margie said. "This puts those same restrictions on your son in spending the money. But that does mean that all of the income taxes will have to be paid at the time of inheritance."

Turning Inherited Retirement Accounts Into a Financial Dynasty

"So," Mr. Alford began, "I have to choose between the potential tax benefits and possibly having my son squander the money, or I can choose to have the income taxes paid all at once and then what's left can be preserved so my son doesn't squander it. Is that right?"

"Well," Andy said glancing at Margie for a moment, "we do have a third option. An IRA Trust can be created. This special trust receives the retirement account money and the trustee would actually be forced to stretch the funds over time for your son. You get the restrictions and the tax benefits. Let me tell you a little more about it…"

With an inheritance for certain beneficiaries, there may be a few concerns about the beneficiary being able to take all of the money out whenever they want. Most couples will trust that the survivor would not be wasteful in using the funds and will do what they can to allow the funds to grow as much as possible. However, the concerns may be far different when talking about other beneficiaries, such as children, nieces and nephews, or other younger beneficiaries.

Whenever assets are placed into an Inherited IRA account, the beneficiary can stretch the payments over their lifetime, but they can also simply take all of the money out in a short period of time. Will these beneficiaries do what is most responsible, or will they succumb to temptation and spend, spend, spend? Unfortunately, just using an Inherited IRA account leaves this decision up to the beneficiary. Fortunately, there is a way to restrict these inherited funds so that the beneficiaries *will* do the right thing—An IRA Trust.

There are substantial tax advantages to stretching a retirement account, but there are no age or other restrictions allowed on an Inherited IRA Account. On the other hand, there are substantial benefits to withholding inheritances for most underage beneficiaries, since it is likely they would waste it, but traditional trusts with age restrictions that are recipients of retirement account funds will have all taxes due immediately. Until recently, there has been a weighing of the pros and cons in choosing potential tax benefits with the risk the beneficiary will not do the right thing versus age restrictions and being forced to pay the income taxes up front. But now there is an IRA Trust that can give the best of both worlds for the end beneficiaries.

An IRA Trust is specially designed to be the recipient of most retirement accounts since it contains specific terms and conditions to allow the funds to grow tax-deferred into the future. The main stipulations contained in this trust are:

- The trust will be the owner of the Inherited IRA Account (after the death of the original owner and during the life of the beneficiary), and the trustee will control all of the investments and distributions of the account assets

- The Inherited IRA Account must distribute the Required Minimum Distributions, but they are distributed to the trust and not to the beneficiary

- All of the distributions out of the Inherited IRA Account are income taxable to the beneficiary

- The terms of the trust determine when the beneficiary actually receives distributions, and until that time the trustee can continue to hold and re-invest funds in other, non-tax deferred investments

It is critical that these and other qualifying language acceptable to the IRS be included in your IRA Trust. To be sure, consult with an attorney who can use the IRA Trust provided by Legis, Inc. (www.legisinc.com).

The trust is the owner of the Inherited IRA Account

As a qualified recipient of inherited retirement account funds, the IRA Trust itself will be the actual owner of the Inherited IRA Account… not the beneficiary. This places the chosen trustee squarely in the driver's seat when it comes to handling all investments and distributions of account funds. If the beneficiary wishes to have money from the trust, then they must go through the trustee to get it. While this can be altered to make some or all of the Required Minimum Distribution amounts actually be received by the beneficiary, this is not necessary. However, it is extremely typical to at least give the beneficiary the amount necessary to pay their added income taxes caused by the Required Minimum Distribution each year.

In addition, it is up to the trustee to decide what kinds of investments will be held in the Inherited IRA Account, including but not limited to stocks, bonds, savings accounts, and just about any other liquid asset. In this sense, the trustee is able to adjust the appropriate investments to best suit the beneficiary. As is typical with most retirement accounts and other investments in general, when people are younger they are able to absorb more risk in their investments and possibly make much higher gains. As people get into their senior years, protection of principal is more important and so more conservative investments are called for. The main point is that these decisions are left to the trustee and not the beneficiary.

The Inherited IRA Account must distribute the Required Minimum Distributions to the trust

The Inherited IRA Account is owned by the trust and governed by the trustee, but the trustee must at least take out the Required Minimum Distribution each year. While this money must come *out of the Inherited IRA Account*, it does not mean that it has to be distributed out *to the beneficiary*. In fact, one of the most attractive points in the IRA Trust is that these distributions can continue to be held by the trust and placed into other traditional investments.

For example, if $350,000 is being held in the Inherited IRA Account during the first year and the IRS guidelines call for $17,500 to be distributed out of that account, the $17,500 can be taken out of the Inherited IRA Account and then invested in a brokerage account in the name of the IRA Trust. The IRA Trust will now own two accounts: the Inherited IRA Account and a brokerage account. Whether or not any of the actual distributions get to the beneficiary is up to you as the creator of the trust, and if you leave no specific guidelines, then it is up to the discretion of the trustee you have chosen.

Because of the potentially strong retention powers held by the trustee, you can see how irresponsible spending can be curbed. But do not feel that such a harsh line needs to be drawn. It is actually far more typical that people creating IRA Trusts encourage the trustee to give the full amount of the required minimum distribution to the beneficiary each year and then only exercise their discretion to decide whether or not to give more if asked. But it is good to know that you can place strong restrictions on a beneficiary if giving the money would do more harm than good.

All of the distributions out of the Inherited IRA Account are income taxable to the beneficiary

Another important point regarding the Inherited IRA Account is that all of the investments in it will grow completely income tax deferred. All income generated by the investments in the Inherited IRA Account are not taxed, and all capital gains are not taxed. They simply stay in the Inherited IRA Account and grow without paying any taxes. However, every dollar that comes out of the Inherited IRA Account when it is distributed to the trust is taxed as income (at the beneficiary's rate). It is this benefit of continual tax-deferred growth of the principal attractive.

For example, if there is $500,000 in an Inherited IRA Account held by the IRA Trust, and those funds are in a mutual fund that has $15,000 in dividends and $17,000 in capital gains, there are *no taxes on the dividends or capital gains*. However, if the Required Minimum Distribution that year is $12,500, then $12,500 is added to the taxable income of the beneficiary. Again, the key point is how much money comes out of the Inherited IRA Account and not what the dividends or capital gains are. Dividends and capital gains are irrelevant.

The terms of the trust determine when the beneficiary actually receives distributions

There is considerable flexibility in determining when a beneficiary actually gets their hands on IRA Trust assets. Whatever terms and conditions you choose are what governs the distributions to the beneficiaries. As mentioned before, most choose to allow all of the required minimum distributions to go to the beneficiary, but that is not required. The only true requirement is that the tax-deferred Inherited IRA Account must give up the Required Minimum Distributions and pay income taxes on it. It does not even matter if the Required Minimum Distributions actually get to the beneficiary or if they stay locked up in the non-tax deferred portion of the IRA Trust.

Many people also choose a set age when the beneficiary gets actual control over the trust and can directly order the trustee to give them funds. Because this trust is usually used as a supplement to income during working years and as a main part of funding retirement, many people choose the projected age of retirement to give control to the beneficiary. This is typically age 65, give or take a few years.

Finally, the IRA Trust becomes irrevocable when the person setting it up passes on and the funds go into the trust. The trustee is then in control of everything. If the beneficiary gets into financial trouble, gets sued, or goes through a divorce, the trustee can lock up those assets until the problems are resolved. So not only is the beneficiary protected from their own potentially bad financial decisions, but their IRA Trust inheritance is also protected from creditors and other legal actions.

You can see there are substantial benefits to Inherited IRA Accounts, and a specialized IRA Trust (again available through attorneys who work with Legis, Inc.; www.legisinc.com) that can help with younger or spendthrift beneficiaries while still retaining special tax-deferred growth across a second generation. For most, these benefits are enough. Having only the required minimum distributions come out of the Inherited Individual Retirement Account allows the remaining funds to grow, and grow, and grow tax deferred. But with the IRA Trust, it can get actually be even better. Because there is nothing that says the required minimum distributions have to go to the beneficiary... only that they come out of the tax deferred account. What happens if most of those distributions are reinvested?

Chapter Five:
Maximizing The IRA Trust

"Thanks for meeting with me," Tara said, shaking hands with Andy and Margie, the attorney and financial advisor. "My father always spoke highly of both of you, but I'm sorry that this is the first time I'm meeting with you in person, Margie."

"I completely understand," Margie said. "Andy has been keeping me up to date with settling your father's trusts. Everything has been taken care of over the past month."

"Yes, it was very quick and easy," Tara said. "According to Andy, the revocable living trust did exactly what it was supposed to do, and now half of my father's retirement account money is in the IRA Trust for my brother. I just have a few concerns about being the trustee of those trusts."

"What concerns do you have?" Andy asked. "You've done a great job getting things organized so far."

"Yes, but the concern is more about my brother," Tara said. "You know he is not very responsible with money. Dad made me trustee with a lot of discretion to protect my brother. Since Dad died, he's started drinking again, and he was addicted to drugs at one point. I'm just afraid..."

"That giving him money may start that habit again," Margie finished. Tara nodded yes.

"The revocable living trust does give you a lot of discretion," Andy said. "You can hold the money back if you feel it's best for your brother. There's no question of that."

"What I'm concerned about is the IRA Trust," Tara said. "Don't I have to give him the, what did you call it, the minimum distributions, each year?"

Andy and Margie smiled. "Actually, no, you don't," Andy said. "For as long as you think Andy is unable to handle the finances, as long as he is in any kind of financial trouble, and certainly if he is back using drugs, you can hold it back."

"And even if you don't think that, you can still hold the money back until Andy is 65," Margie said. "The Inherited IRA account is inside the IRA Trust. The required minimum distributions have to come out of the account each year. They don't have to leave the IRA Trust and go to your brother. They can actually be reinvested in other accounts inside the IRA Trust. This will actually give your brother a lot more money to retire on when he does turn 65."

Tara sat back and smiled. "Well, my brother is not going to be too happy right now," she said. "But hopefully he'll be a lot happier when he's 65."

There are substantial advantages in having an IRA Trust set up to manage an inherited retirement account for a beneficiary who may be overly tempted to withdraw the money early. And with some studies showing about ninety percent (90%) of inherited retirement account money being spent in two years, there is a high probability that without an IRA Trust the funds would be gone in short order.

While the IRA Trust automatically puts decisions on distributions in the hands of your chosen trustee, many trustees may be tempted to simply give the beneficiary all of the required minimum distribution. They don't have to. The money can instead be reinvested inside the trust.

Choosing an age to turn over control

In determining an age of "responsibility" for inheritance purposes, many attorneys advise their clients to look back to their own past and think of how they would have spent the money at a certain age… and then add five years.

In imagining an appropriate distribution age, most people currently see ages between 25 and 40 as appropriate. At 25, most people have either gone through a four year college or university, and then they had a few years to get established. If they did not go through college, they have still had a few years to get established in their own careers. Twenty-five seems to be the age, currently, of starting to get serious about life. On the other hand, the age of forty seems to be the age where if they have not gotten their act together, they probably won't ever, so why hold up the distributions?

The days of 18 or 21 being a reasonable age to turn over an inheritance are gone, despite the laws considering 18 year olds full adults. As life expectancies increase, it seems that people figure they have more time to grow up. But these ages of inheritance are generally for use in Revocable Living Trusts or Wills, and not for IRA Trusts. With an IRA Trust, there are more opportunities for high-impact growth and retirement security, and so different ages are desirable.

Most people creating an IRA Trust jump forward to an age limit of 65 years figuring that is an appropriate age of actual retirement. So even if the beneficiary did no retirement planning of their own, they will still have a substantial retirement when the time comes. So at 65, the trustee turns control of the trust over to the beneficiary. Until then, the trustee decides when and how much money to put into the actual hands of the beneficiary.

The "Practical" Annual Distribution

The trustee does not have to give the beneficiary any funds until they reach the age chosen by the person setting up the IRA Trust. However, there are annual tax implications that go along with assets growing inside the IRA Trust.

- Income taxes have to be paid on the required minimum distributions that come out of the Inherited IRA Account each year.

- If money that comes out of the Inherited IRA Account is reinvested in stocks or mutual funds, then the dividends and capital gains taxes have to be paid each year.

The reality is that the IRS does not care who pays the taxes as long as they are paid. So the two options are to have the trust pay these taxes each year or have the beneficiary incur the taxes and pay them each year. However, trust income tax rates are much higher than individual income tax rates, so it is best to have an individual pay the taxes.

But where is the beneficiary going to get the money to pay the taxes?

The practical solution is for the trustee to offer to pay the accounting fees to prepare the beneficiary's taxes each year and then distribute just enough money so the trust pays the "difference" in taxes between what the beneficiary actually has to pay and what they would have paid without the "extra" income from the trust. The trustee can then also offer to give the beneficiary a little extra money each year.

For example, let's assume that Trustee Tara wants to assign her brother Roger the beneficiary all of the income and capital gains taxes but doesn't want to give her brother anything more than she has to. If her brother's tax bill without the trust income would be $13,500 but with the trust income his tax bill jumps to $18,500. Tara can arrange with her brother to pay an accountant to prepare the income taxes for Roger, pay the "extra" $5,000 for the additional income taxes, and then give Roger $1,000 to do as he pleases.

Tara can now let the additional income from the Inherited IRA Account and other account gains be reinvested to grow even more next year.

The "other" investments

The additional investments inside the IRA Trust can be anything legal. Brokerage accounts, mutual funds, CDs, annuities, and even plain old savings accounts can be used inside the IRA Trust outside of the Inherited IRA Account. Basically, if it can be used as an investment, then the IRA Trust can hold it.

However, there are three things to keep in mind about these "other" investments. First, these investments are not tax-deferred. While everything inside the Inherited IRA Account is tax-deferred, nothing inside the other investments is tax-deferred solely because it is inside the IRA Trust. There may be certain tax-deferred investments that can be used, but keep in mind that if you owned an account yourself and would have to pay income or capital gains taxes on it, then there would still be income and capital gains taxes on it inside the IRA Trust.

Second, unlike the Inherited IRA Account, the required minimum distribution rules do not apply to the other investments. The tax rules that force a minimum amount to be taken out each year do not apply to the other investments, so they can stay in and grow as long as desired.

Finally, the other investments do not necessarily count as income when they are taken out of their account. Every penny that comes out of the Inherited IRA Account is taxable income. But this rule would not apply to the brokerage accounts, mutual funds, or money market account investments.

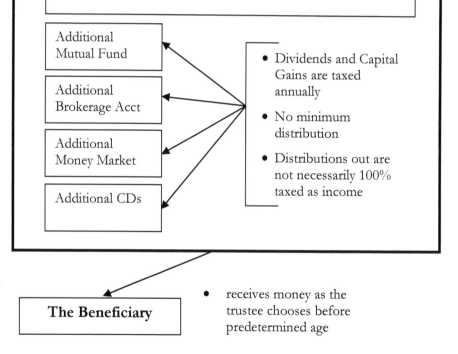

IRA Trust

- Trustee manages all assets
- Trustee decides when money goes to beneficiary before predetermined age

Inherited IRA Account

- Investments grow without taxes on dividends or capital gains taxes
- Required Minimum Distributions must come out of the account each year
- No income taxes are due when the money goes into the Inherited IRA Account

Additional Mutual Fund

Additional Brokerage Acct

Additional Money Market

Additional CDs

- Dividends and Capital Gains are taxed annually
- No minimum distribution
- Distributions out are not necessarily 100% taxed as income

The Beneficiary

- receives money as the trustee chooses before predetermined age

As a word of caution, each investment has its own tax liabilities and possibilities. Make sure to discuss each investment with a qualified and reputable financial advisor before investing.

Summary

There are substantial opportunities for beneficiaries to grow inherited retirement account money, but beneficiaries do not necessarily do the right thing. While some beneficiaries may not make the right choices with an inheritance, some may simply not have the best information to make these choices. Having the right IRA Trust in place can maximize growth of their inheritance, provide protection from creditors and divorcing spouses, and provide them with a sizeable retirement of their own. Again, to be sure you have the right trust, consult with an attorney who works with documents prepared by Legis, Inc.

Made in the USA
Las Vegas, NV
17 May 2021